Dictionary of Dogs

Use the alphabet to find out all about dogs.

by Susan Piper

abcdefghijklmnopqrstuvwxyz

800-445-5985
www.etacuisenaire.com

Dictionary of Dogs
ISBN 0-7406-4133-6
ETA 382141

ETA/Cuisenaire • Vernon Hills, IL 60061-1862
800-445-5985 • www.etacuisenaire.com

Series © 2006 by ETA/Cuisenaire®

Original version published by Nelson Australia Pty Limited (2002). This edition is published by arrangement with Thomson Learning Australia.

All rights reserved. No part of this publication may be reproduced, stored in a retrieval system, or transmitted, in any form or by any means, electronic, mechanical, photocopying, recording, or otherwise, without the prior written permission of the publisher.

ETA/Cuisenaire
Manager of Product Development: Mary Watanabe
Creative Services Manager: Barry Daniel Petersen
Production Manager: Jeanette Pletsch
Lead Editor: Betty Hey
Copy Editor: Barbara Wrobel
Production Artist: Diana Chiropolos
Graphic Designer: Amy Endlich

Photograph on p. 9 courtesy of Guide Dog Association of Victoria
Photograph on p. 9 courtesy of Melbourne Greyhound Association
Photograph on p. 11 courtesy of Di Mannering
Photograph on p. 13 courtesy of Gaston Vanzet
Photograph on p. 28 courtesy of RSPCA Victoria

Teacher consultant: Garry Chapman, Ivanhoe Grammar School

Printed in China.

06 07 08 09 10 11 12 13 14 15   10 9 8 7 6 5 4 3 2 1

abcdefghijklmnopqrstuvwxyz

Alsatian [al-SAY-shun]

A large, intelligent breed of dog, often used for police work or as guard dogs. These dogs are also called German Shepherds.

breed

A group of dogs that have a similar look and character.

Bulldog

Border Collie

These are all breeds of dogs.

Spaniel

canine [KAY-nine]
1. Anything to do with dogs.
2. Any of the animals in the dog family, including wolves, jackals, and foxes.

canine tooth
One of the four pointed teeth on either side of the upper and lower jaws. These teeth are large in dogs.

collar

A band, usually made of leather, that is put around a dog's neck. A name tag can be attached to the collar. A leash can be clipped to it.

coat

The layer of fur that covers most dogs.

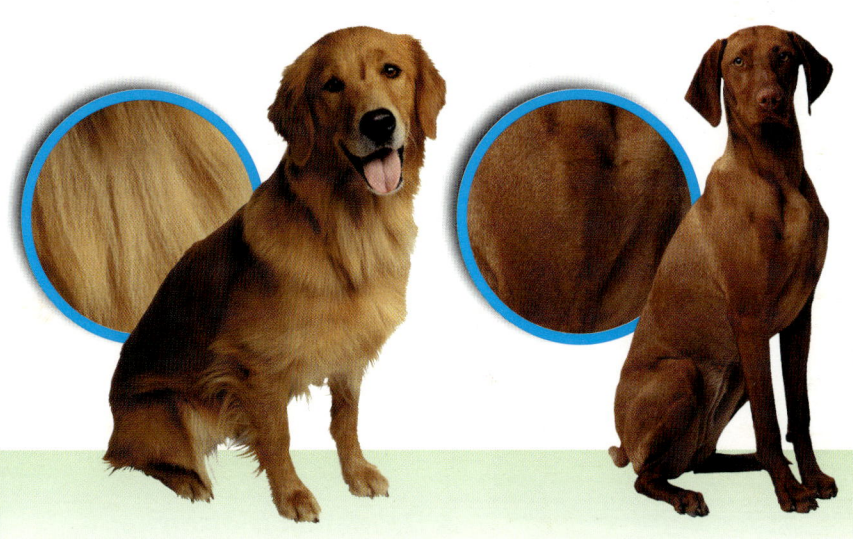

Retrievers have long coats. **Vizslas have short coats.**

Dalmatian
[dal-MAY-shun]

A breed of large white dog that is spotted with black or dark brown marks.

A Dalmatian is often kept as a pet in a fire station.

ears

The part of the head that is used for hearing and that has large covering flaps on most breeds of dogs.

A dog can hear sounds that people cannot.

flea

A small, blood-sucking insect that lives on dogs and other animals. It is able to make big leaps.

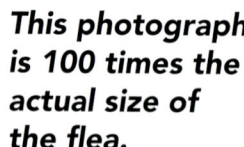

This photograph is 100 times the actual size of the flea.

fox

An animal related to dogs. It has upright ears, a pointed snout, and a long bushy tail.

Greyhound

A tall, thin breed of dog that is able to run fast.

guide dog

A dog that is specially trained to lead or guide a blind person.

hunting dog

A dog that is used to help people catch or kill wild animals.

Husky

A breed of dog from the Arctic. It has a thick coat and is often used to pull sleds as part of a team of dogs.

Irish Wolfhound

A large hunting dog from Ireland.

The Irish Wolfhound is the tallest breed of dog. The Chihuahua [chi-WAH-wah] is the smallest breed.

jackal

A wild dog that lives in Asia and Africa and hunts at night in a pack.

According to legend, jackals help lions hunt and kill other animals.

Kelpie

A working dog bred in Australia to look after and round up sheep.

kennel

A small crate or house for dogs.

Labrador

A breed of large dog with a short black or golden coat. It makes a good pet or guide dog.

leash

A strap or chain with a loop at one end and a clip at the other. It is attached to a dog's collar to keep the dog in check.

mongrel (also mutt)

A dog of no particular breed.

Mongrels combine the characteristics of several breeds.

abcdefghijklm**n**opqrstuvwxyz

name tag

A disc attached to a dog's collar with information about the owner.

Old English Sheepdog

A big dog with a shaggy coat. It was originally used to herd sheep and cattle to the markets in English country towns.

Although Old English Sheepdogs are big, they are gentle and make good pets. They do need lots of space and exercise, though.

pack

A group of canines that live and hunt together.

Poodle

A breed of dog with thick, wiry hair that is often clipped into different shapes.

"Poodle" comes from the German word for "splash," because the Poodle is a water dog.

quadruped
[QUA-druh-ped]

An animal that has four feet.

✓ *These animals are all quadrupeds.*

✓ horse

✓ sheep

✓ lizard

✓ cat

✗ *These are not quadrupeds.*

✗ *People are bipeds (two feet).*

✗ *Spiders have eight legs.*

✗ *Beetles and other insects have six legs.*

Retriever

A hunting dog that has been bred to pick up dead and injured birds and bring them back to the hunter.

Retrievers have coats that dry quickly. They are good swimmers, and have a keen sense of smell.

scent

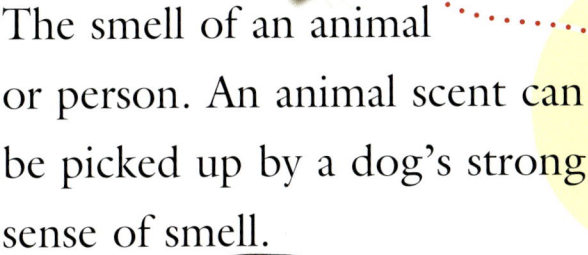

The smell of an animal or person. An animal scent can be picked up by a dog's strong sense of smell.

St. Bernard

A large dog with a good sense of smell. It is famous for being able to follow the scent of lost people in cold and snowy conditions.

tail

The end part of a dog that can be wagged. Dogs use their tails to let you know how they are feeling.

When dogs are happy, they wag their tails.

Terrier

A breed of small dog originally bred for hunting.

vet (short for veterinarian)
A doctor who takes care of animals.

Vizsla

A Hungarian sporting dog bred to hunt birds and small animals, such as rabbits.

wild dogs

The many different types of dogs that live in the wild, including the African Wild Dog, the coyote [ki-OH-tee], and the Australian Dingo.

African Wild Dogs are common in southern Africa. They hunt grazing animals, such as gazelles and zebras.

Wolves live in a wide range of environments from the snowy regions of North America to the deserts of India.

wolf
A large, wild dog common in India and North America.

X-ray

A special photograph that shows the inside of the body.

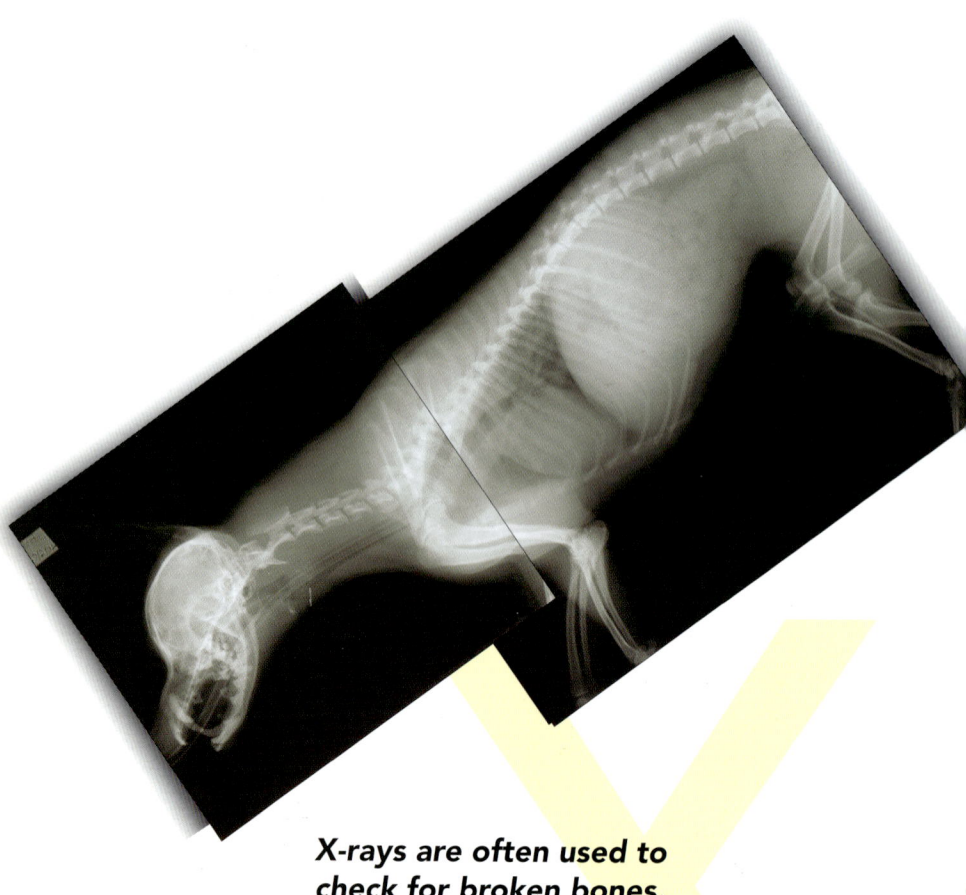

X-rays are often used to check for broken bones.

Yorkshire Terrier

A small dog with long hair. It was originally bred in the north of England to hunt rats and mice.

abcdefghijklmnopqrstuvwxyz

zebra

A horse-like wild animal with stripes. Zebras live in Africa and are hunted by African Wild Dogs.

African Wild Dogs hunt in packs. They single out an old or sick animal from a grazing herd and chase it until it can run no more. Then they attack.